The Birthday PARTY Planning Guide

How To Quickly And Easily Plan Your Child's Perfect
Birthday Party And Create Memories
That Will Last A Lifetime

Pete Gradows

Writing & Publishing Process by PlugAndPlayPublishing.com
Book Cover by Tracey Miller | www.TraceOfStyle.com
Edited by Lauren Cullumber

ISBN-13: 978-1530007523

ISBN-10: 1530007526

I dedicate this book to all of the parents
who have invited me to their parties.

Pete Gradowski

Acknowledgements

To Steve Dolan, who helped me get off the ground with my first website, and his patience with my ever-changing design ideas.

To The Bay Area Group. From letting me film in your houses, to showing up at the theater shows. Thank you for cheering me on with the next project.

To Ma and Pa, thanks for having faith in me when I took the big leap. And no, you still can't be my manager.

To Malinda, for cheering me on and putting up with all of my shenanigans.

To Jimmy Lucarotti, for your constant patience and helping me spitball crazy ideas. You're my best friend, man. Thanks for giving me a pat on the back with every hurdle and challenge.

To Weston Lyon, for molding my words into coherent thoughts, and for keeping me on track. You've been awesome to work with and have made this so effortless.

And finally, to Frank and Evan, for giving me something to push against to succeed.

Pete Gradowski

Table of Contents

Introduction

What you're about to dive into is a step-by-step process for throwing a stress-free party, enabling you to create memories for your child that will last a lifetime. I've left no stone unturned. This isn't a haphazard Google search on party themes (though there is an entire chapter on that on page 3), or activities (those, too, have a chapter, beginning on page 13). Your time is valuable, so I owe you more than that.

You see, instead of leaving you to the wolves to cobble together a list, I'm giving you the insights that most parents don't have. Because I've attended many, many birthdays, I'm going to cut the learning curve for you.

Here's how I've laid this book out for you: there are 14 chapters. Each chapter covers a basic element of a party, followed by examples, and tips for activities for different age groups. In certain chapters, I have an additional "Pete's Party Planning Point," covering ideas that most people don't think about.

I know your creative juices will be flowing while you read this book, so I've included a "Notes" section on page 44 that you can use to jot down any important ideas for your next party (or another party in the future). My goal is for you to reference this book every year.

In addition, I've included a party-planning checklist on page 41 to make this process even easier for you!

While the emphasis here is on planning ahead for a party, I understand you may be putting together an event at the last minute. If this is you, I recommend turning to page 39 for a bonus chapter on last minute ideas.

To get the most out of your planning, I suggest reading through this book and trying to use as many ideas as you can. Take notes and use this book to plan the best possible party with the time you have. You'll be able to use this book to plan great parties for years to come!

Alright, let's get to it.

Date and Theme

Planning your party 4-6 weeks in advance is best. Just as in school, waiting until the last minute to "cram" usually results in failure. Choose a few dates around your child's actual birthday (the weekends before or after, and maybe even a little further out on either side are great options). **If your child's best friend is not available on the date you are considering, choose another date.** Celebrating with their "partner in crime" is a bonding experience, and also gives your little one some calm if things become too hectic.

Pete's Party Planning Point

Some extended family may not be able to attend. This is your child's day; ask him if he'd like them to attend. This is another reason why planning ahead is critical.

Weekend parties are better for younger children and sometimes make it easier for family to attend, while older children often enjoy an after school party, if you can manage it. The entire group will love spending all day in anticipation of going home together, plus your party won't clash with a weekend sport or activity. If you are planning a weekend party, keep in mind that many sports have games on Saturdays, and some people attend church in the morning or evening on Sundays.

The Tag Team Party

Does your child have a good buddy with a birthday in close proximity? Team up to reduce effort (and scheduling) for all! At a field day themed party, the two birthday boys can choose teams for the day, and compete during the various games. With an added stake of who'll reign supreme, the friendly competition also allows bragging rights. Having a tug of war or water balloon toss are some great party ideas, but we'll get to that in the next chapter.

Pete's Party Planning Point

A Tag Team Party is best reserved for children seven and older, as younger children rarely want to share the spotlight. While planning with other parents can make a tag team party easier to plan, keep in mind there might not be the same overlap of friends.

We'll go through a sample party day outline in a later chapter, but here's a quick snapshot based on your child's age.

The following time frames will apply to most party formats:

Childs Age	Party Time Frame
1-3	Late morning (10 AM or so) until about 1 PM (depending on naptime)
4-6 or 7	12:00 PM until 3:00 PM, which allows plenty of time for games, food, and socializing
7 and 8-10	Early Afternoon from 1:00 or 2:00 PM to 4:00 or 5:00 PM
10-13	Later afternoon into evening. These are generally events like sleepovers, drive-to location (e.g. Jungle Island), pool parties, or arcades.

Theming

Alright, his best friend is on board and the grandparents are available. What now? Referencing the time frame guidelines, let's dive into some ideas...

Children ages one to three are often over stimulated with all of the attention and commotion. Some cultures honor a first birthday with a lot of reverence. These parties can be quite large, with some renting large community halls and having extended family come from out of the area (and sometimes from out of state) for the special event.

Of course, that's not always necessary or practical. If you know other parents from day care, "Mommy and Me" type groups, or from around the playground, a quiet day in the park can be just as fun. Whatever avenue you decide to pursue, remember that the children may become over stimulated. Be sure to allow for a separate area or mellow/cry room to take them to if it becomes too much.

Children in the four to six, and young seven-year-old crowd are very excited to hang out with friends from school. For a party focus, ask about a favorite movie or TV show, which can make decorating easy. But be sure to ask them for their input. They love to be involved with the process. You can plan surprises and games, but they get to choose the theme, characters, etc.

Depending on the season, finding a local park to host the party in will allow the group some fresh air, plenty of room to be rambunctious, and more importantly, keeps your house clean. This might result in a theme being streamlined and minimized to balloons, cake, napkins and plates. This isn't a bad thing. Hanging out with their friends and a simple tie-in will suffice.

If you do decide to host the party in your home, let your inner artist go crazy! One party I attended, the theme was Harry Potter. Dad was dressed as Professor Snape, and bottles of soda had

Butterbeer labels applied to them. The kids were running around outside playing Quiddich with brooms, and broom parking signs were on the front porch. Mom was a muggle in awe. By using streamers with the Harry Potter color scheme and having the soundtrack playing inside throughout the party, it was very cohesive and not terribly expensive.

Another inexpensive yet wildly successful theme was a celebrity/fashion based party. Chairs were set up in front of a backdrop of a white sheet. A bucket of props were left in front, forming a makeshift photo booth. This mom said she raided the dollar store and found some neat things like plastic glasses, boas, canes, and other fun odds and ends. The pictures made a nice party favor.

For the seven to ten crowd, plan a LOT of activities. Some might run at the same time. While some guests might want to run around and play, others may gravitate towards something more

Pete's Party Planning Point

You can create and share playlists on your smartphone. Some options you can check out are Pandora, iTunes, and Spotify.

How to get started with Spotify:
1) Sign up. Like most apps, you can sign up easily through Facebook. A quick note here: if you DO sign up using Facebook, check the default settings and unclick "share" notifications or any of your friends will know what you're listening to.
2) Choose your plan (prices as of this writing vary from free to $9.99/month)
3) Once you are logged in on your desktop, click on Preferences
4) To import your music, go to Local Files, select the folder(s), and click OK.
5) Once the files are imported, click on "New Playlist," give it a name, and you're all set.

low-key, such as coloring. **Children around this age can be introverted, so plan activities that let them participate but won't have the spotlight on them.**

When you ask your VIP what theme they have in mind, be prepared to forge ahead with different ideas. This is also the age range when they will want to help you decorate the room(s) with signs, posters, balloons, etc. If the theme is a favorite movie, play the DVD in the background, or as an activity while you wait for everyone to arrive. Include costume accessories in goodie bags. A lot of bakeries (and supermarkets are getting hip to this now, too) can print a picture, logo, or character onto the cake.

This is also the age range when your child owns the party. No longer willing to just sit and be pampered, this is when kids want to ensure EVERYTHING has been taken care of, and double checked.

The classics are always popular theme ideas. For boys, timeless guaranteed winners are pirates, superheroes, Star Wars, and Disney.* For girls of this age, it's Disney, faeries, and heavy on fantasy. Be prepared with games and activities. Friendship bracelets, crafts, and team building activities are a safe bet.*

Ask your child if they would like this to be a costume party. That Halloween costume can get a second life with a little creativity.

Pete's Party Planning Point

As with the younger crowds, have a separate room for the birthday child or guests that get overwhelmed. It can be challenging for parents to plan and run a party. But it can be equally draining for the birthday child to be the center of attention.

Here's another successful party example. I performed for a crowd consisting of a gaggle of eight-year-old boys. The whole family loved to cook. Food Network was a staple in their home and food was treated as a religion. The party was centered on baking, and everyone made their own personal pizzas from a toppings bar in the kitchen, followed by an ice cream sundae from a separate toppings bar in the back.

Remember the Harry Potter party mentioned earlier? The muggle mom asked me to collaborate due to the obvious tie-in to magic. Music from the soundtrack was sprinkled throughout the show (and any attempts to deviate were met with pleas to change it back). The children received wands in their goodie bags. With plenty of lead time, I can work seamlessly with your theme and ideas (no matter how off the wall they may be).

The ten to thirteen year olds have a different idea of a party. It can often become an all-day event. Older kids tend to want to get a change of scenery. Hanging out with their friends becomes the focal point. Successful party ideas include a pizza and movie out-ing, and an "all in one" location, such as Jungle Island. Miniature golf locations can also host a group with golf, food, and drinks. Prices vary, but they do not have to be expensive.

Another WILDY clever party I recently performed at was "drive-in theater" based. A projector was connected to a laptop and the movie was shown on the side of the house while blankets were put on the driveway and grass. The parents' cars were in the driveway to act as a back wall behind the group, and the parents walked around with concessions.

Location, Location, Location

In every neighborhood, amongst the group of friends, there is always one house where everybody goes to hang out. They may have the coolest video games, be the only house with a pool, or just have parents who are cool. These hangouts have a "home away from home" type of energy.

My house was not that house. Yours may not be either. When planning the location of the party, consider whether your home is kid friendly.

Some pros to hosting the party at your home include:

- You get to control the environment.

- The birthday child may be more comfortable on their home turf.

- It makes invitations and directions easier (versus an outdoor party, for example…more on that below).

- Snacks, meals, cake, etc. can be made ahead of time and put in the fridge.

- Easier to plan games and activities, and you have more flexibility with entertainment.

- When all of the guests have left, a quick clean up and everyone can relax and go to their rooms. (No traffic, car seats, etc. to contend with).

If you decide your home or apartment isn't suitable for a children's party, there are several offsite options that come with obvious advantages (including being able to come back to a clean home after the children have been picked up).

9

For a small fee, you can often reserve space in a community recreation center or local park. This is a good idea if you are planning to have a lot of children attend. Ask a few parents to stick around and help out. Potlucks are a good idea here.

Local parks are also a great go-to location. Some even have barbecue pits and picnic tables. Some require reservations, which guarantees your location and lets you get the other party elements together ahead of time. Others have a first come, first served policy. Depending on weather, the season, etc., I've seen families camp out very early in the morning to get these unreserved spots.

Some pros for throwing a party outside:

- Parks with playgrounds let kids burn off a lot of energy until the activities begin.

- You can come home to a clean house.

- Kids thrive on a change of scenery, and the party becomes an experience.

Other options to consider are classics. Kid-friendly restaurants, such as a favorite pizza place, or hands-on museums (in San Jose we have The Tech Museum and the Children's Discovery Museum).

Pete's Party Planning Point

Parties away from home usually work better for children over five since younger children may be overwhelmed by unfamiliar surroundings.

There are also the self-contained venues such as Chuck E. Cheese, Golfland, and Jungle Island. These venues will do most of the heavy lifting for you, but make reservations ahead of time, as weekend dates are VERY popular (if they are booked, consider a Friday evening or special day after school).

Prices can add up as well. Depending on the size of the crowd you're anticipating, the amount of planning you're willing to invest, and your budget, these types of hotspots are classics for a reason.

Fun Birthday Ideas & Activities by Age Group

Children like to share. If you plan a game for your party, your kids might want to play it with other friends at school, and vice versa. Plan enough time for the kids to play outside in the back yard, or (like at many parties I perform for, depending on space) run around inside the house.

As mentioned earlier, if your house is lived in and not a museum with valuables, then playing tag indoors might work for you. However, if you set up dividers, (i.e. outside is for run amok time and inside is for organized games, cake, and behaving ourselves), this can work.

Younger children like to be hands-on and kept busy. Finger painting and coloring sheets that are consistent with your party theme (you can copy pages from a coloring book) are great options. There are so many theme varieties, add-ons, and tie-ins to choose from. I'm reminded of a parent who had a simple "Lego building hour." If you try this idea, perhaps offer small prizes for the most creative, most consistent with the theme, or best team sculpture.

Preschool children enjoy simple party games, movement, and art activities. It's helpful to plan the activities with your child. Consider mural painting, dance games, or a cooking project.

Kindergarten and elementary school children will probably have more elaborate birthday party ideas and activities in mind. If finances permit, consider an activity-heavy party. A party where children make puppets and perform a puppet show is a fun option and not too costly. All you need are some socks or paper bags and some markers and stickers.

Older children may request a sleepover birthday party. Consider whether this is something you would like to supervise, recognizing that you probably won't get much sleep. That said, a sleepover with a small group can be a wonderful, close time for children that they'll remember for years.

Need birthday party ideas that span different age groups? Children of all ages enjoy being creative. Consider decorating party hats, making picture frames (be sure to put in a group photograph of the children at the party), or having children decorate their own cupcakes or cookies.

Scavenger hunts are great fun for kids. The level of difficulty can be raised or lowered depending on the age of the children. They can also be adapted to the rest of the decorations and activities throughout the day (pirate treasure hunt, a princess finding her white knight scavenger hunt, even a Fall/Halloween scavenger hunt). Simply make sure that there are prizes for all the children.

If weather does not permit, or if you just want to keep them contained in one place, you may also consider having the children play detective, with clues placed throughout the house or venue. Write five or six clues and place the first one in an envelope. If your child has a favorite item in the house, this is a great opportunity to highlight it. The clues can vary in difficulty. I was asked to create clues for my nephew and I hid them too well (one clue was for a remote control and I placed it inside the battery compartment). Depending on how many children attend, you may break the "super sleuths" into teams. Magnifying glasses and notebooks (available from a dollar store) make great party favors.

Hiring Entertainment

When hiring ANY entertainer, gather references from other parents as well as children's museums or local libraries. Yelp is also a great resource. Before you invite anyone into your home, make sure you see a video or two of their performances.

Also, a rule that is often skipped is: **ask your child if they want an entertainer**. Watch the performance videos together. This allows your child to pick someone they like, and will feel comfortable with on their big day. It all goes back to working together to ensure a great party. When you call a potential entertainer, ask what age group the show is designed for before you mention your child's age. That way you ensure it is a good fit. No entertainer is perfect for all ages. If you will have kids in different age groups attending, focus on the median age, or the age of your child. It's their big day.

1. I know I'm biased, but there is a reason why magicians are a classic for kids' parties. This is the age when they want to interact, they believe in magic, and it fosters creativity and imagination. Ask the magician if they have a special highlight trick (the child floats, or is made to appear, for example). A magic show also provides a lot of volunteer opportunities, which means more photos for your gallery.

2. Balloon artists are becoming popular. Their creations double as party favors. Watching a requested animal/sculpture take shape in front of their eyes is a joy to see.

3. Mobile petting zoos are available regionally. This will depend on your budget, and prepare to pay for the quality ones. While some may be on the lower cost side, they usually do not treat their animals well. You might not be able to get your child the pony they want, but this is the next best thing. Best

of all, this experience will have the children talking about it for quite some time.

4. If your children like to dance and move, consider a choreographer or dance teacher. Many can be found at your city's community center. Live ballet, hip-hop, or silly dancing are great activities and allow the whole group to participate. After the "class" everyone can get their groove on with a huge dance party.

5. Face painters are also a hit with children. Best reserved for outside or in a rented venue, many can accommodate theming (superheroes, princesses, etc.). Unlike full-face masks or paint, each cheek presents a clean slate for a new idea. (Have a mirror or two and a camera ready!)

6. Costume characters have been a popular choice for a long time. This is a GREAT idea tied to the overall theme. If your child has a favorite TV or movie star, they will love to meet them in person. Being able to meet the star, take pictures and interact with the character's show will give your child memories LONG after the party.

Pete's Party Planning Point

Plan ahead, especially for the costume character companies. Many use unlicensed characters. Disney is VERY serious about their characters, so Mickey or Elsa may look odd, as there are no official costumes for them. Again, always ask to see videos of performances.

One parent couldn't seem to decide on entertainment, and so they offered a double feature of magic and superheroes. Not only did the heroes look, well..."funky," their music and show were not at all appropriate for a six-year-old's party.

If you are a member of your school's PTA, you can ask other parents for suggestions. A quick Google search can also provide a network of parent groups or forums, and neighborhood message boards.

A final note on entertainment: a professional entertainer's job is to not just provide a service, but also to make your job easy. They are guests at your child's party, and should be honored to be there. Being self-contained, upfront with expectations and time frames, and allowing you to focus on the next activity is part of their job. Don't let them forget this.

Pete Gradowski

Guest List

You may be asking yourself "How many kids should I invite?" The general rule, often ignored, is: your child's age plus one. That means four friends for a 3-year-old's birthday. For toddlers, it's best to invite at least one friend he or she sees a lot and feels comfortable around. (If your child goes to daycare or preschool and is used to being with a large group of kids, she can probably handle a few additional guests.)

On the other hand, grade-schoolers have definite ideas of whom they want to invite, so you can use the opportunity to teach them to be considerate of others' feelings. Explain why inviting 10 out of 12 kids in the class is bad form. Better to invite everyone and hope for some no-shows. Inviting 4 out of 12 kids, however, is more a matter of discretion and will work better if the bash isn't held immediately after school. In that case, the invitations should then go out by snail mail or email, which we'll discuss next.

Teach your child not to talk about their upcoming party around those she didn't invite (and then cross your fingers). Be sure and write your first name on the invitation so guests who RSVP won't have to ask for "John's mom."

Pete's Party Planning Point

Ask for RSVPs, but don't worry about stragglers. It's always handy to know how many people are going to show up at your party, especially when guests arrive with siblings. But a few RSVPs are bound to get lost in the parenting chaos. Plan on a few extra portions of food and don't worry about it.

Invitations

If you have embraced a character-based party, a visit to a local party supply store will provide invitations, napkins, party favors (more on that a little later), and cups, plates, etc. Or, you can cobble it together yourself. (The dollar store is great for decorations and invitations, as well.)

While creating your invite list and sending out the invitations, there is a risk of invites getting lost in the mail, or recipients forgetting to return them to you. But with an online invitation service such as Evite (which I highly recommend), you can guarantee almost immediate replies.

Let's face it: people check their emails on their phones. The ability to simply open and tap "yes I'll attend" makes it easy for your guests, and easy for you to get a daily update on a head count.

Evites in a Nutshell

Evite makes online invitations easy. You will need to register, and you have the option of manually inputting the email addresses you want to send to, or you may import them.

Evite makes this VERY simple and walks you through, step-by-step. It even sends party reminders automatically! By leaving little guesswork for you, and making it easy for other parents, I think this is the safest bet. There's no reason to make things more frustrating than necessary.

Last, avoiding food allergy mishaps is important. You don't want to find out after an allergic reaction that one of your party guests can't eat nuts or gluten. So, I recommend asking for any dietary restrictions when people RSVP. That way, you can plan your party menu accordingly.

Food

For brief parties, cake and ice cream is really the only refreshment you need. Many young children look at the cake as the focal point of the whole birthday ritual, so be sure to let them help make it (or select it from the bakery).

At a party I performed at recently, they had a Mad Hatter theme. On the "snack table" there were various teas, finger sandwiches, and cookies. The kids wrote "drink me" on the cups, and "eat me" on their plates. This worked better than children writing their names on cups, as they got to personalize and could recognize their own handwriting.

Cake

Depending on the age of your child, you might want to forgo baking a cake, and order something simple from a favorite grocery store the day before. Gaining popularity at a lot of parties is ordering a small decorative cake and then supplementing with cupcakes. For some reason, a lot of kids will choose cupcakes over cake every time. Of course, children like to decorate their own cupcakes. With a small toppings bar/buffet, this crosses two items off the list at once: a fun activity and snack time.

Tradition dictates that the birthday boy or girl gets the first piece of cake (and that they will probably choose the piece with the most frosting and decorations on it). Since young children can be picky eaters and may prefer ice cream over cake, you might consider having more than one flavor of ice cream on hand. Older guests may actually enjoy preparing the food as much as eating it, so consider substituting cooking for a craft.

Munchies

Throughout the party, kids will get hungry and antsy. Between the main meal and cake, provide the little ones with things to snack on. The less complicated the party dish, the less you have to clean up later.

One really cool idea I saw at a backyard barbecue party was a "Tacos in a Bag" snack. Essentially, you brown your protein of choice the night before or morning of the party. Prep the fixings buffet style. Hand every child a bag of tortilla chips (Doritos, Fritos, etc.) have them add their toppings and protein and the bag acts as a shell. No spills, fun to make and eat, and EASY clean up.

You'll also want to offer a variety of foods. Ordering a few pizzas takes care of the main course, but think about including fruit, nuts, cheese, crackers, or popcorn for snacking.

When it comes to beverages, you don't need to buy bottles of water or cans of soda. Try using pitchers of water (with cucumbers or fresh fruit inside) and make a creative lemonade punch that can be served from glass dispensers or pitchers.

Supplies

Create a party box. The best time to pick up decorations is after a holiday (Halloween, Christmas, Valentines Day, etc.).

You will be able to buy colorful wrapping paper or decorations at rock bottom prices. Considering that you will likely use one roll or decoration per party that you host, buy 2-3 of each item, so you're not kicking yourself later, wishing you had an extra to spare.

Get a large storage container to store each seasonal themed set of decorations, and label appropriately. As you stock up, you'll notice that a lot of items have universal applications (i.e. a broom from Halloween can be used at a Harry Potter themed party).

Have a generic party box stocked with supplies most people forget. Some supplies may include balloons, birthday candles, a lighter or matches, batteries, the cake knife, a permanent marker, pen and paper, and scotch tape in it. Put your children's names on cups with a permanent marker. This will save on paper supplies.

Pete's Party Planning Point

Don't forget about Pinterest. Why reinvent the wheel? There are TONS of decorations, recipes, and theming ideas, updated almost daily.

If you're looking for inspiration, users have pinned every aspect of every conceivable celebration. While you need an account (and registration is super easy), you can get around that by doing a Google search with "Pinterest _____" (filling in what you need help with).

When it comes to tablecloths, plates, napkins, and cups, keep it cheap. You can buy plain colored party items from the dollar store.

And once you establish a theme for the party, rummage through your local thrift shop for hidden treasures. A birthday mom and I got to talking about thrift store shopping, and she said she found great items for a little girl's tea party themed birthday at a local thrift store.

She got two sets of teacups and dishes that totaled around $20 for both sets. She also found tablecloths, big hats and fancy umbrellas for a low price.

Goodie Bags

You don't need to spend a lot of money to have a successful party. This is a party for your child and her friends — not for other parents. Save the fireworks display for your next adult gala. The kids just want to play.

Controlling expenses also means that you should not feel obligated to send home goodie bags full of expensive toys. While some stickers with characters from the party (pirates, superheroes, etc.) or a craft make nice souvenirs, parents agree that it's time to start saying no to elaborate party favors.

Kazoos, bracelets, and plastic puzzles may be junk to us, but they're treasure to a 4-year-old. Stick to your guns and a budget, though. Any more than $5 per goodie bag is ridiculous.

Think outside the bag, as well. How about sending everyone home with a packet of seeds to plant in the garden, or some colored modeling clay? Another example of a low-cost, fun, and interactive party favor came from a mom with a huge patio. She handed out a small box of colored sidewalk chalk to everyone at

the end of the party. Most kids sat right down to draw on the patio.

You can host a drawing contest, or create a sidewalk mural where all the children get to contribute. Take a picture and email it or print it as a favor. The total cost for all this bliss? Ninety cents each.

Putting the Puzzle Together

It's time to connect the dots. You know how many children are coming (allowing for a few stragglers), the cake is in the fridge, and the games and craft stations are prepped. Now what?

It's time to set the agenda for the day. Now is not the time to "wing it." Kids can be unpredictable, and you don't want all of your prep work to be in vain. Here is a sample outline…you can tweak, fill in, or remove as needed.

Sample Outline (Based On A Party Starting At 1:00 PM)

10:00 AM: Gather all of the games, crafts, and activity supplies. Set up different station/activity areas. Distinguish "no entry" rooms (kids love to explore, so make sure they know what rooms are off limits).

If you have pets, you may need to put them outside for the party. An older sibling or parent can check in on them and keep them company, as all of the stimulation can make pets anxious, as well.

If you are making food, prep the food now. If ordering food (pizzas, sandwiches, etc.), make sure you have the contact number ready.

11:00 AM: Begin setting up decorations, and talk to the birthday child about what to expect. Let them know it's their big day, but set up the ground rules.

Your child's friends might misbehave at a house that is not theirs. When rules or discipline need to be enforced, you may need to discipline them, but hearing it from your child reinforces your message, and helps soften the blow.

12:00 PM: Set up a "get to know you," first arrival activity. This can be playing outside, a jumphouse, etc. As children begin trickling in, they will look for the party to start.

Put any snacks out, and place them closer to the center of the table. Rambunctious energy may knock food and drinks over.

Make sure you have a time-flexible activity. Also, while the party start time is on the RSVP, plan for some early arrivals, and, more frequently, late arrivals. Getting children fed, organized, and prepped, plus traffic, can get a family WAY behind. So try to be flexible. However, remember: the party doesn't officially start until your child's best friend arrives.

1:00-ish ("ish" is the operative word): Once a majority of the guests arrive, this is the time for the first activity. This is also a great time for snack time. If you have hired an entertainer, they should check in at least 30 minutes early to get set up. If you don't think you'll hear your doorbell or knocking on the door, perhaps have a sibling or your spouse be on the lookout for arriving guests. Or, have a sign saying, "Party is in the back," or "Come on in."

2:00 PM: This is a great time for the entertainment or show. If you have opted for an activity that will take awhile (photo booth, craft, scavenger hunt, etc.), now is the time for it.

At this point most of the children are in the party groove,

so take a lot of pictures here. If you are ordering food, order it at this point as well.

3:00 PM: LUNCH TIME. This is best in a separate corner/ space than the other activities. Allow plenty of time for the kids to catch up and hang out.

4:00 PM: Time for cake. This is the highlight of any party. If you're planning to have your child open presents during the party, this is the time to open them (more on presents later). Keep a list of who gifted what. This helps with thank you cards later. Take plenty of pictures.

5:00 PM: Time to wrap things up. Goodie bags and a final activity while parents begin to pick up their children.

6:00 PM: Take a deep breath, and give yourself a high five. You did it!

Presents

Some parents are on the fence about whether their child should open presents at the party. I side with the parents in the "no" camp.

Opening gifts can send already excited kids over the edge, resulting in a frenzy of torn paper, discarded cards, and hurt feelings about slighted gifts. Opening presents after the party means you get to avoid all of the above. It also extends the celebration for the birthday child and allows him to wind down a bit before tackling a pile of gifts (and you get to keep track of who gave him what!).

However, most kids will tell you that opening presents is one of the best parts of a party (next to the cake). In the end, it's up to you to decide.

Take into account the size of the gathering, the kids' ages (children under four are less likely to be able to sit through opening a slew of gifts), your own child's personality, and the current level of chaos.

Pete Gradowski

Thank You Cards

They're a gracious touch, and learning this early is a nice idea. Young kids can draw a picture of the present, then you fill in the words yourself. An older child can sign his name and, by age 6, should be able to write his own note. Don't worry about the spelling.

Pete's Party Planning Point

Remember to have fun. The party is the main event, but what you're really doing is creating memories for your child. Yes, parties are work, but don't be afraid to ask for help from other parents or a spouse. Take a day to relish in the "post-birthday party glow," but remember what you learned when planning for next year's party

Conclusion & Free Party Gifts

I know this has been a lot to process. Parties are meant to be fun, but they can sometimes be a pain to plan. That's why you read this book. So, hopefully you've picked up a few tricks to make the party planning process easier, and dare I say, even enjoyable.

If you still have questions or concerns, or need a little help in the party planning process, shoot me an email at Pete@PeteGmagic.com. I'm happy to help.

In fact, no matter where you are in the planning process, I'll team up with you for a 10-minute birthday party consultation, where you can pick my brain and we make sure you're going in the right direction.

NOTE: This is only available to purchasers of this book, so be sure to mention the "Party Planning Guide" in the subject line.

Last, just like any good party, this book includes a SURPRISE! If you are thinking about hiring entertainment, as a free gift to you, I'd like to send you a special report on "The 10 Things Every Performer Should Do To Help Your Party Shine."

If you're interested in this free, surprise gift, simply shoot me an email at Pete@PeteGmagic.com and mention "Surprise Gift" in the subject line.

I hope you enjoyed this book, and I look forward to seeing you at a party soon!

Pete G

PS - There are some last minute details MANY parents forget, so I've included a Bonus Section on the next page (and a party planning checklist on page 41). Enjoy!

Bonus Section

Here are some last minute ideas to keep in mind on the big day.

Which house is yours?

Some parents may not have been to your house before. Neither has the entertainment. It's always a good idea to put a few balloons on the mailbox. If your house is hard to find, and GPS might not suffice, include any necessary directions in the RSVP.

Parking

It's always a good idea to give your neighbors a heads up that you are planning a party. Especially if it is on a Saturday or Sunday afternoon. Parking can be a hassle. If a parent is only dropping off a child, then they can stay close. Otherwise, ask parents to drop them off and park a little further away. Some parents may only stay a little while. As convenient as it may be, do not double park. There is nothing worse than talking to someone and then being asked to move to let another car in or out.

Stop the Screen Syndrome

This is a touchy subject. Ask parents to tell their children to leave their cell phones at home. Or at least put them on a table until cake/presents/picture time. When one child has their phone out, they check out of the party. Once one phone is out, they all come out. The focus is on honoring your child on their big day. Selfies during the cake/presents are ok. But break the screen zombies free!

If there is not a local party store close by, here's an even better decoration choice.

I love Oriental Trading Company. Their seasonal decorations, free shipping (over a certain amount, or you can find free shipping coupons online as well), and variety are great. They offer entire backdrops, decorations, party favors, and costumes. If you'd like to dedicate your entire house to the party, the cost is reasonable and many items can be re-used for other themed parties.

Who Can You Tag In?

Depending on the scope, size, and guest list, you may need help. Is a sibling going to lead a game? Who is going to order and pick up the food? Are any parents staying at the party with their child? Other parents want to ensure their children have fun, and if they get to be a part of the process, they usually will.

Birthday Party Planning Checklist:

6 Weeks Before

[ ] Choose a theme with your child

[ ] Determine the guest list

[ ] Reserve your party venue and hire a party entertainer

4 Weeks Before

[ ] Prepare your invitations

[ ] Ask for an updated class list from your child's teacher

[ ] Determine games, activities and menu to match your party theme

[ ] If ordering a cake, place your order

[ ] Mail invitations

[ ] Purchase party supplies, especially if ordering online

[ ] Arrange for extra help, if necessary

1-2 Weeks Before

[ ] Create a party flow schedule

[ ] Purchase more party supplies as needed

[ ] Call families who have not yet responded to your invitation

3 Days Before

[ ] Purchase food

[ ] Collect items for party box (cake knife, candles, lighter, etc)

[ ] Call entertainer to confirm appearance and expectations

[ ] Call party venue to confirm all details

[ ] Assemble party favors

1-2 Days Before

[ ] Bake a cake or pick up pre-ordered cake

[ ] Confirm help if using extra help

[ ] Decorate home or gather decorations for party venue

[ ] Prepare make-ahead food

1-2 Days After

[ ] Send Thank You Notes!

About the Author

Pete Gradowski, aka Pete G., has performed magic professionally all over the Bay Area since 2000. He's consulted on various sized parties, from small birthday get togethers to events where the sky's the limit.

Along that journey he has cultivated tips and determined the key factors that make the difference between a smooth, stress-free, FUN party vs. a party that runs the hosts into the ground.

With thoughtful planning, kids' birthday parties can be meaningful occasions of joy and celebration with limited stress for the grownups.

For more information about Pete G. and how he can help you create an unforgettable birthday party experience for your child's birthday party, please visit www.PeteGmagic.com.

Notes

Notes

_____

_____

_____

_____

_____

_____

_____

_____

_____

_____

_____

_____

_____

_____

_____

_____

_____

_____

Notes

Notes

_____

_____

_____

_____

_____

_____

_____

_____

_____

_____

_____

_____

_____

_____

_____

_____

_____

_____

CPSIA information can be obtained
at www.ICGtesting.com
Printed in the USA
LVOW04s1557140616

492562LV00013B/599/P